Lunch Around the World

BY LOUISE FRANKLIN

T0306541

NATIONAL GEOGRAPHIC LEARNING | CENGAGE

It's noon. It's time for lunch.
What do people eat for lunch?

People like to eat different things.
Lunch is different around the world.

UNITED STATES

peanut butter and jelly sandwich

BRAZIL

bolinhos de bacalhau

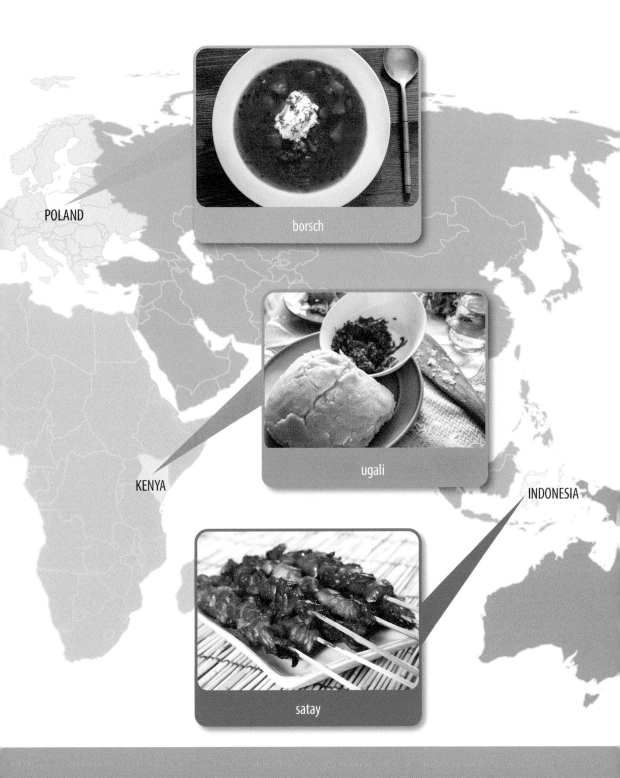

POLAND

borsch

KENYA

ugali

INDONESIA

satay

People around the world eat burgers.
Are all burgers the same?

U.S.A.

India

No, they are different!

U.S.A.

INDIA

bun

meat

hamburger

bun

potato

vada-pav

Some people make lunch.
Some people buy lunch.

Mateo is from Guatemala.
He likes empanadas.

empanadas

How much does an empanada cost?

It costs two quetzals in Guatemala.

It costs $3.00 in the United States.

2 quetzals

$3.00

Tasuku is from Japan. He likes beef and rice. Beef and rice is called *donburi*.

donburi

JAPAN

How much does donburi cost? It costs 500 yen in Japan. It costs $7.00 in the United States.

500 yen

$7.00

Lilya is from Russia. She likes chicken and mashed potatoes.

mashed potatoes

chicken kotlety

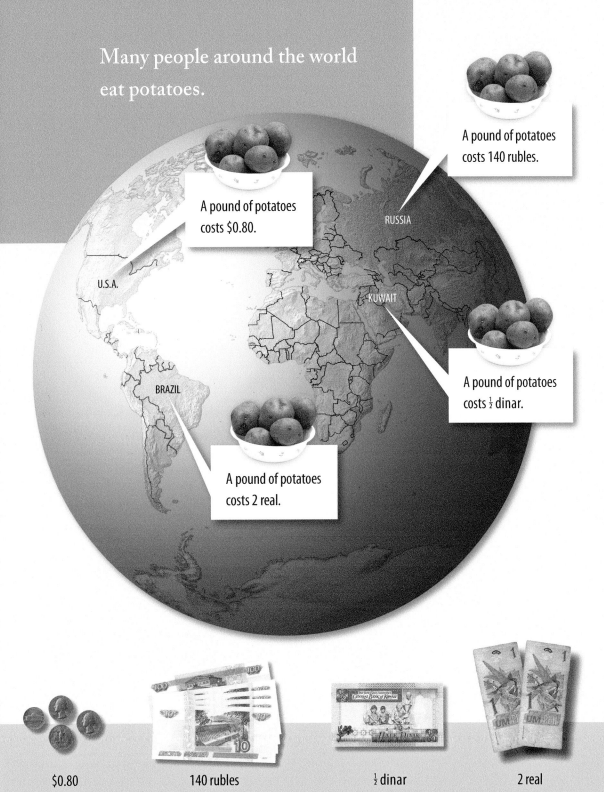

Many people around the world eat potatoes.

A pound of potatoes costs 140 rubles.

RUSSIA

A pound of potatoes costs $0.80.

U.S.A.

KUWAIT

A pound of potatoes costs $\frac{1}{2}$ dinar.

BRAZIL

A pound of potatoes costs 2 real.

$0.80

140 rubles

$\frac{1}{2}$ dinar

2 real

Eva is from Costa Rica. She likes rice and beans. Rice and beans is called *gallo pinto*.

gallo pinto

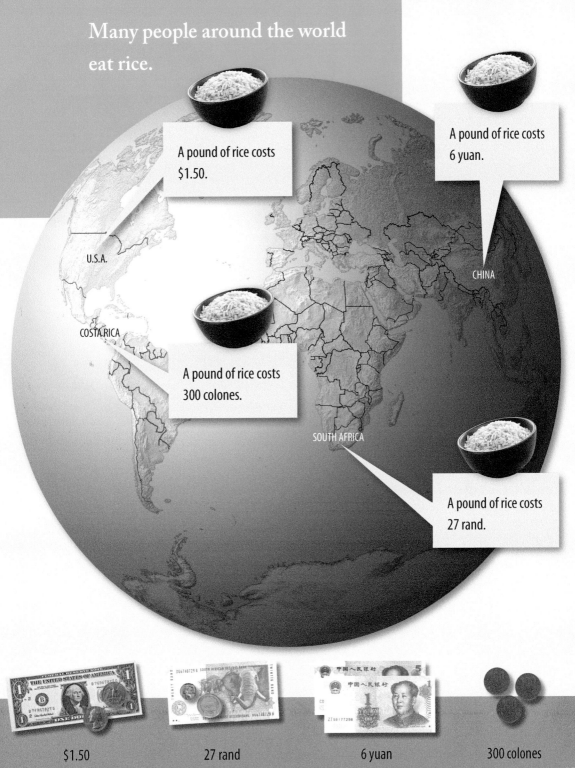

Many people around the world eat rice.

A pound of rice costs $1.50.

A pound of rice costs 6 yuan.

A pound of rice costs 300 colones.

A pound of rice costs 27 rand.

U.S.A.

CHINA

COSTA RICA

SOUTH AFRICA

$1.50   27 rand   6 yuan   300 colones

Lunch is different around the world.
But everyone likes to eat lunch!

It's noon. What do you like to eat?